LITTLE RED RIDING HOOD

A Pantomime in a Prologue
and Three Acts

by

K. O. SAMUEL

SAMUEL FRENCH

LONDON

NEW YORK SYDNEY TORONTO HOLLYWOOD

FOR AMATEUR PRODUCTION ENQUIRIES

UNITED KINGDOM AND WORLD
EXCLUDING NORTH AMERICA
plays@samuelfrench.co.uk
020 7255 4302/01

Each title is subject to availability from Samuel French,
depending upon country of performance.

CHARACTERS

The Fairy Queen.

The Witch.

King Wolf.

Simple Simon.

Red Riding Hood.

The Baron.

Mrs. Hubbard.

Punch
Trunch } (two Village Constables).

Prince Charming.

Dandy.

Gamekeeper Wood.

Splinter (his Assistant).

A Footman.

Fairies, Villagers, Hikers, Guests, etc.

SYNOPSIS OF SCENES

LITTLE RED RIDING HOOD

PROLOGUE

Scene.—*A woodland glade.*

The Curtain *rises on* Fairies *dancing. After the dance, the* Fairy Queen *enters and comes* c.

Fairy Queen. Fairies, salute your queen!

(*As the* Fairies *form a quick tableau, with suitable gestures of welcome, the* Fairy Queen *watches their movements critically.*)

Your steps are improving, but when you strike attitudes you must have grace—(*she illustrates as she speaks*)—and, above all, poise. If you wobble, you spoil everything.

(*One* Fairy, *unable to maintain her pose, wobbles dangerously and is frowned at by the* Fairy Queen.)

But I haven't come to give you dancing lessons. There is other work to be done.

(*The* Fairies *break the tableau and gather round in an attentive group.*)

The wolves in the forest are getting overbold and are a menace to certain of our mortal friends. These wolves must be tamed.

Fairies. We're afraid of the wolves!

Fairy Queen. You, Fairies, afraid of the wolves! You've all been served out with wands; why don't you use them?

1st Fairy. I met a wolf in the wood. As he came round a bend

I waved my wand at him and he bit off the end !
    (*She cries.*)

FAIRY QUEEN. You didn't wave it properly.
There is an art in waving a wand. (*She illustrates
with her own wand.*)

    2ND FAIRY. I met a wolf as he was coming out of
      his lair.

I—I—was so frightened—I vanished into thin air !

FAIRY QUEEN. You mean you—faded out ?

2ND FAIRY. I'm afraid so. Safety first, you know.

FAIRY QUEEN. He was probably just as frightened
of you.

    3RD FAIRY. I met a wolf—I didn't know *what*
      to do.

I was terribly scared—so away I flew.

FAIRY QUEEN. Your wand would have protected
you.

3rd FAIRY. I—I—hadn't got it with me.

FAIRY QUEEN. That's no excuse. You know
our orders. When on duty in the forest, wands
will be worn ! (*She looks round.*) Any other *brave*
encounters ?

    4TH FAIRY. I met a wolf—his tongue hung out
      and his eyes gleamed.

I'm afraid I completely lost my nerve and I screamed !

FAIRY QUEEN. It really looks as if the wolves are
going to have it all their own way. And *that's* going
to be very bad for somebody.

FAIRIES. For somebody ?

FAIRY QUEEN. Yes, for poor little Red Riding
Hood. By the way—(*she looks at her wrist as if to
see the time*)—isn't it her usual time for passing
through on her way to Grandma ?

5TH FAIRY. We haven't seen her yet, but we've
seen the Prince. He's out hunting to-day.

FAIRY QUEEN. Ah, the Prince ! Such a charming
man !

FAIRIES. Yes—Prince Charming !

(*They all laugh.*)

Fairy Queen. I often wonder why he's still a bachelor. I think we ought to find him a sweetheart.

1st Fairy. What about little Red Riding Hood ?

Fairy Queen. Yes, she might do. She's *very* pretty. Really, I think that's an excellent idea. Yes, Prince Charming shall marry little Red Riding Hood. (*She moves* ʀ.)

(*The* Witch's *cackle is heard off stage and she enters up* ʟ. *almost immediately.*)

Witch. That shall never be !

(*The* Fairies *huddle in a frightened group round the* Fairy Queen.)

Fairy Queen. Nobody asked for your opinion, old Witch. You weren't invited.

Witch. If I waited for invitations, I should never get anywhere. (*She laughs.*) But I go where I like and I say what I like, and I say Prince Charming shall never marry Red Riding Hood. King Wolf wants her—and with my help he'll have her.

Fairy Queen. Not while the fairies are on her side.

Witch. Fairies ! (*Long laugh.*) Fairies you call them ! (*She points a derisive finger at the group.*) They *look* very nice, but they don't *do* anything. They spread their little wings and they wave their little wands—and what happens ? Why, nothing happens ! (*She cackles hoarsely at her joke.*) Nothing happens ! But when I use my magic powers quite a lot happens, as you will see.

Fairy Queen. We'll fight against you—now and always.

Witch (*shrieking*). I defy you !

(*The* Fairy Queen *laughs at the* Witch, *who becomes enraged.*)

If it's to be war, then let's begin it.
I'll boil my soup—and you'll *all* be in it !

Fairy Queen. We've heard those threats before,

old Witch. You make a lot of fuss about your wonderful soup, but when it *does* boil—what happens ? (*She laughs as she uses the* Witch's *words.*) Why— nothing happens !

Fairies (*echoing her words and laughter*). Nothing happens !

(*Exit the* Fairy Queen *and* Fairies r. *The* Witch *comes down* c.)

Witch (*muttering to herself*). We shall see, we shall see. (*She has brought her crystal with her and she now discloses it to the audience, whom she proceeds to take into her confidence.*) And what shall we see ? Witches, in their crystals, as you know, Invented television years ago. Now we can see, as clear as clear as day, What's taking place not very far away.

(*She gazes into the crystal and then proceeds in the manner of a running commentary.*)

Ah ! see ! There is little Red Riding Hood, tripping along the woodland path, carrying her basket of eggs and butter for Grandma. She is singing to herself. She little knows what is in store for her. (*She chuckles.*) King Wolf is hiding behind a tree, waiting to spring out on her. (*She peers more closely into the crystal.*) Yes, I can just see his long snout sticking out from behind the tree. Red Riding Hood is getting nearer and nearer. Now she is only a yard or so away. Ho ! Ho ! King Wolf has sprung out from his hiding-place. Red Riding Hood sees him. She gives a cry of fear !

(*There is a cry off stage. At this point in the* Witch's *commentary appropriate sounds off stage should illustrate the action she relates.*)

She drops her basket. (*Crash off stage.*) King Wolf seizes her. They struggle. (*Sounds of struggle off stage.*) Ah, what is this ? What is this ? (*The* Witch *utters a cry of rage.*) That Fairy Queen is inter-

fering again. She's arrived at the critical moment.
She hits King Wolf over the head with her wand.
(*Loud crack off stage.*)   He sinks to the ground with a
groan. (*Groan off.*)   Red Riding Hood picks up the
fallen eggs, puts them back in the basket, one by one
(*this sound can be made by the orchestra*), and hurries
off. King Wolf rises and limps away, howling. The
sound of his howling dies away in the distance.

(KING WOLF *is heard off stage, howling, beginning
    faintly, but getting louder and louder until, as the
    WITCH puts her crystal away, he makes his entrance
    up L. as if just recovering from his encounter with
    the FAIRY QUEEN, as described by the WITCH. KING
    WOLF should not be played too heavily. He is
    boastful in the manner of Falstaff. He wears a skin
    and a crown on his head which has a tendency to
    slip sideways. He walks upright and his mask
    should enable him to speak clearly.*)

KING WOLF. Foiled again! Foiled again! To
think that I had that little girl in my clutches and
let her get away!
WITCH. Yes. So we noticed. Red Riding Hood
is not to be caught that way. I've told you that
before, but you still keep on trying.
KING WOLF. That miserable Fairy Queen! She
hit me a crack over the head with some blunt instru-
ment. (*He takes off his crown, breathes on it and
polishes it with his paw.*)
WITCH. Yes, quite a crack. We heard it from
here.
KING WOLF. I'll call out my pack and have her
torn to pieces. (*He replaces the crown on his head.*)
WITCH. King Wolf, the sooner you realize what
you are up against, the better. That sort of talk
won't get you far.
KING WOLF. But the girl! Little Red Riding
Hood! I must get her somehow. She's such a
succulent morsel! I gnash my teeth when I think of
her! (*He begins to whimper.*) Help me, Witchy!

Dear Witchy ! (*He gives the* Witch *a weak, imploring hug.*)

Witch (*consoling him*). Now, don't break down. It's too early. (*She gags.*) We haven't got through the first act yet.

King Wolf (*beginning to sob*). Help me, Witchy !

Witch (*patting him*). There, there ! Put your hat on straight.

(*She straightens his crown, brings out a large handker-chief, wipes his eyes and holds it to his nose, and says, " Blow."* King Wolf *blows his nose noisily and feels better.*)

Now, listen to me and I'll tell you a secret.

(King Wolf *jumps away and makes a great business of peering at all exits to see that nobody is listening.*)

There is a scheme afoot to marry Red Riding Hood to Prince Charming.

(King Wolf *leaps in the air and makes gestures of rage.*)

Now don't get excited. I haven't finished yet. Put your hat straight. (*Business with crown again.*) I don't know why you want to wear this thing at all. There's not much of the *King* about you.

King Wolf. And there won't be much of the *Prince* about the Prince when I've done with him.

Witch. I will prevent the marriage, never fear. I have enough power to forbid the banns. (*She chuckles.*)

King Wolf. What will you do ? Tell me—before —before I do something rash ! (*He leaps about the stage, beating the air with his paws.*)

Witch. Not so fast, King Wolf, not so fast. Give me time to lay my plans and you shall have your little Red Riding Hood.

(King Wolf *goes into transports of joy, seizes the* Witch *by the waist and whirls her round in an ecstatic waltz.*)

Now be off with you and leave me to my schemes.

(*She beats him with her stick and he blows her a kiss, still waltzing by himself, and exits up* L. *The* WITCH *comes* C., *shaking with laughter.*)

My magic now has only just begun.
I'll fool them one and all before I've done!

CURTAIN.

ACT I

SCENE.—*The village of Merryvale.*

On the R. *is* MOTHER HUBBARD'S *house entrance, bearing the sign : " Ye Olde Cupboarde." There is a window over the entrance.*

A chorus of DAIRYMAIDS *is discovered, singing and dancing, after which* SIMPLE SIMON *enters from up* L. *His shirt-sleeves are rolled up and he carries a bucket.*

SIMPLE SIMON. Good morning, Milkmates !

(*The* MAIDS *stampede towards him and he is nearly buried in the rush of welcome. The bucket is dropped and rolls away.*)

What's all the fuss about ?
MAIDS. You !
SIMPLE SIMON. Me ?
1ST MAID. Yes. It's so nice to see a man about the place.
2ND MAID. And you're the only unmarried man in the village, you know.
SIMPLE SIMON. I suppose that's why they call me Simple Simon.
3RD MAID. It's time you gave up being so simple.
SIMPLE SIMON. But then I shouldn't be Simple Simon. Have you heard my signature tune ?
MAIDS. No ! Sing it to us.
SIMPLE SIMON (*singing*). Simple Simon met a pie-
      man
Eating his curds and whey.
He put in his thumb and pulled out a plum,
And so the poor dog had none.

1st Maid.   I think that's silly.
Simple Simon.   Well, I can't alter it now.   It took me two weeks to learn that.
2nd Maid (*sidling up to him*).   A great big chap like you ought to be thinking about getting married.
Simple Simon.   I haven't got time.   I'm much too busy.   And that reminds me—where's my bucket ? Somebody's kicked it.

(*A* Maid *retrieves the bucket and gives it to him.*)

I've got to give the place a wash and brush-up. The Prince will be here at any moment.
Maids.   The Prince !
Simple Simon.   Yes, haven't you heard the news ? The Prince is out hunting to-day and he's coming here, so you'll all see him.

(*The* Maids *crowd round* Simple Simon *excitedly.*)

And what's more—he's going to stop here for lunch.
Maids.   The Prince !   How exciting !
Simple Simon.   Yes, he's ordered Ye Olde Lunche at Ye Olde Cupboarde, and if you want to make yourselves useful you can go and pick some of Ye Olde Flowers to put on Ye Olde Table.   They do say he's very fond of pretty things.
1st Maid.   I'll pick a special bunch for the Prince myself.
2nd Maid.   And so will I.
3rd Maid.   And so will I.
Simple Simon.   And so say all of us.

(*The* Maids *run off up* l.   Simple Simon *walks towards the house, singing, "* And so say all of us,*" etc.   The* Baron *enters up* l.)

Baron (*catching sight of* Simple Simon).   Ha ! Hi !   You !
Simple Simon (*not understanding*).   Ha hi yu ?
Baron (*calling him again*).   Here !   You !   Hi !
Simple Simon (*to the audience*).   He thinks I'm a Chinaman, I suppose.   I'll speak to him in Chinese.

(*He goes up to the* Baron, l.c.)   You want Ha Hi Yu.
Me no Ha Hi Yu.   Me Simple Simon, velly bussy
man, no can fetchee Ha Hi Yu——
    Baron.   Drop that nonsense !

(Simple Simon *drops the bucket.   The* Baron *points to
the house.*)

Is Mrs. Hubbard at home ?
    Simple Simon.   I'll see.   (*He goes to the house and
calls.*)   Mother !
    Mrs. Hubbard (*within*).   Hullo !
    Simple Simon (*to the* Baron).   What name, please ?
    Baron.   Tell her the Baron would like a word with
her.
    Mrs. Hubbard (*within*).   I'm out !
    Simple Simon.   She's out.
    Baron.   She's in !   I heard her voice.
    Simple Simon.   No—that was just an echo.   (*He
calls again.*)   Hallo !
    Mrs. Hubbard (*within*).   Hullo !
    Simple Simon.   You see !   There's no one there.
Mrs. Hubbard's not at home.

(*Enter* Mrs. Hubbard *from the house.*)

    Mrs. Hubbard.   Hullo !   What's all this hulloing
about ?
    Baron (*getting   angry*).   He told me you were
out !
    Mrs. Hubbard.   Well, I *am* out, aren't I ?   What
d'you want ?
    Baron.   I've come about your rent.
    Mrs. Hubbard.   Oh dear me, where is it ?   (*She
looks hastily at her dress.*)
    Baron.   That's just it.   Where is it ?
    Mrs. Hubbard.   Well, I can't see it.   Can you
see a rent anywhere, Simon ?
    Baron.   I don't mean *that* sort of rent.   This is
what I mean.   Read it.   (*He thrusts a paper into her
hand.*)
    Mrs. Hubbard.   What is it ?

BARON (*folding his arms and facing front*).   I have put my demand in writing.

MRS. HUBBARD (*peering closely at the paper*).   Oh, is this writing ?   All this squiggly stuff ?   Fancy that !

BARON (*shouting*).   Read it, madam !

MRS. HUBBARD.   It's very small.   I must put my glasses on.   (*She brings out a large pair of lorgnettes and gazes through them at the paper.*)   No !   I still can't see anything.

BARON (*angrily snatching the paper away*).   I will read it to you.

MRS. HUBBARD.   Now pay attention, Simon.   The Baron's going to read to us.

BARON (*reading*).   " I hereby give you due notice that unless——"

MRS. HUBBARD.   Oh !   Oh !   I say, Baron !

BARON (*alarmed*).   What's the matter ?

MRS. HUBBARD (*still gazing through her lorgnettes*). I can't even see *you* now.   Where are you ?   (*She takes the lorgnettes away.*)   Oh ! there you are.   These glasses are really no good at all.   I must have them altered.

BARON.   " —unless your rent is paid within the week, you will receive notice to quit."

MRS. HUBBARD.   Give me the paper.

(*The BARON hands her the paper, which she tears into pieces.*)

Simon, put these into the insinulator.

(*SIMPLE SIMON takes the pieces and exits into the house.*)

BARON (*stamping   with   rage*).   You   defy   me, madam ?

MRS. HUBBARD.   If I *owed* you money—and, mind you, I've only got your word for it—I say, if I *owed* you money, I don't think I should pay you.   I just— don't like your face.

BARON (*raging*).   Isn't that just like a woman !

MRS. HUBBARD.   Well, I *am* a woman.   And now

let me tell you that I'm expecting Royalty to-day and I can't be bothered with a mere baron, so I give *you* notice to quit—in other words, kindly 'op it !

(*The* BARON *waves his clenched fists above his head in impotent rage, strides* L.C., *and turns at the exit.*)

BARON. There are other means of getting the money and I shall not hesitate to use them.

(*He exits up* L.)

MRS. HUBBARD (*cogitating, hand to mouth*).   Now, I wonder what he meant by that.   Oh, I can't be bothered to think now.   I'm too excited about the Prince.   (*To the audience.*)   Of course, you know why he's coming here, don't you ?   You see, my great-great-great-grandmother was *the* Old Mother Hubbard, and she used to live in this very house. Yes, people come from miles around to see the old original cupboard and the poor dog.   Of course, the dog isn't alive now.   He's stuffed—which is more than he was in Old Mother Hubbard's days !   But the cupboard's kept nice and bare, just as it was when she made her famous journey to get the bone. A rich American came the other day and he was *so* interested that he wanted to take the whole house out to America, piece by piece.   Nursery rhymes were his hobby, he said.   He'd already collected all sorts of relics.   He'd got the original Christmas pie, with the hole still in it where little Jack Horner had put his thumb, and the original shoe that the old woman had lived in, and a leg of Mary's little lamb, and little Miss Muffet's tuffet—yes, he'd got very nearly the whole set, but he wasn't going to have my cupboard and I told him so, in no uncertain voice.   And, talking of uncertain voices, have you heard mine ?

(*Song by* MRS. HUBBARD.)

(*After the song, she exits and returns to the stage, carrying a feather duster.*)   Now I must make everything clean and tidy for the Prince's arrival. (*She looks at the house.*)   The cupboard looks as if it could do with a dusting.   (*She proceeds to dust the wall and door of the house.   When she can't reach up any farther, the window attracts her attention and she pulls out her lorgnettes and gazes at it.*)   Simon! Simon! Drat that boy.   Where's he got to ?

(*Enter* SIMPLE SIMON *from the house.*)

SIMPLE SIMON.   Here I am, Mother.
MRS. HUBBARD.   The window has not been cleaned.
SIMPLE SIMON.   Oh, I never clean *that*.
MRS. HUBBARD.   Why not ?
SIMPLE SIMON.   I can't reach up there.
MRS. HUBBARD.   You can use the steps.
SIMPLE SIMON.   I never thought of that.

(*He goes back into the house.*)

MRS. HUBBARD.   What a boy !   I declare he gets sillier and sillier every day.

(SIMPLE SIMON *enters with a pair of steps, a bucket and a mop.*)

Now hurry up.   You haven't much time.
SIMPLE SIMON.   All right, Mother.

(*He swings the steps round and hits* MRS. HUBBARD *on the back of the head as she goes off.*)

MRS. HUBBARD.   Now then, watch your step.
SIMPLE SIMON.   I have washed the step, Mother.
MRS. HUBBARD.   I said " watch it," not " wash it."

(*She exits into the house.*)

SIMPLE SIMON (*puzzled*).   If I watch the step, how can I clean the window ?   Well, I'd better clean the window first.

(*He can have business here with the steps, bucket and mop.   He goes up the steps, carrying the mop, but forgets the bucket ; comes down again for the bucket and leaves the mop behind ; tries to take them both up together and falls off the steps.)*

Well, perhaps I'd better watch the step instead. Hallo ! Here's little Red Riding Hood.

(Enter RED RIDING HOOD, *carrying her basket. She is excited and breathless.)*

RED RIDING HOOD.   Simon, I've had such a fright this morning.
SIMPLE SIMON *(rubbing his head).*   So have I.
RED RIDING HOOD.   Oh dear, I'm out of breath.
SIMPLE SIMON.   Well, you can't have any of mine. I shall want all my breath for cleaning that window. But what's happened ?

(He picks up the pair of steps and comes C. *to* RED RIDING HOOD. *He lays the steps down and they sit side by side on them as she tells her story.)*

RED RIDING HOOD.   I was attacked in the wood by a horrid wolf ! It sprang out at me from behind a tree and took me by surprise. And then, what d'you think happened ?
SIMPLE SIMON.   You woke up !
RED RIDING HOOD.   It's all as true as true can be, Simon. Look, here are the marks of its horrid sharp claws. I felt its hot breath on my cheek when—suddenly——
SIMPLE SIMON.   You woke up again !
RED RIDING HOOD.   Suddenly it relaxed its hold and sank to the ground with a groan and I looked up, and what do you think I saw ?
SIMPLE SIMON.   Stars !
RED RIDING HOOD *(gazing in front and becoming absorbed in her story).*   A white light——
SIMPLE SIMON.   A night light ?
RED RIDING HOOD.   A white light ! And standing in the white light was a beautiful fairy. Oh, so beautiful ! *(She clasps her hands, rises and comes down* C.) She spoke to me and said that the wolf

could do me no harm because the fairies were watching over me.

(SIMPLE SIMON *rises, picks up the steps and gazes blankly at her.*)

And she said something else, too. She said I was destined to marry a prince !

(SIMPLE SIMON *opens his mouth in astonishment, and starts a backward movement towards the house.*)

I wonder what Mother will say when I tell her.
    SIMPLE SIMON. *I* know what Mother will say. She'll say, " Fetch a doctor ! "

(*He exits with the steps.*)

    RED RIDING HOOD. If only it would all come true !

(*Song by* RED RIDING HOOD, *which takes her off.*)

(*Enter* PUNCH *and* TRUNCH, *the village constables. If possible these should be " the long and the short of it,"* TRUNCH *being the short one and wearing a helmet so large that it covers up most of his face.*)

    PUNCH. Now, Trunch, you know what we're here for, don't you ?
    TRUNCH. No, I don't !
    PUNCH (*aghast*). You don't ! You're a *nice* policeman !
    TRUNCH (*flinging himself at* PUNCH). Kiss me, Sergeant !
    PUNCH (*pushing him away*). Now then, none o' that !
    TRUNCH. You said I was nice.
    PUNCH (*lifting up* TRUNCH's *helmet*). Your helmet's too large for you.
    TRUNCH. I know. I'm going in for promotion.
    PUNCH. Promotion ?
    TRUNCH. Yes. I'm expecting a swelled head.
    PUNCH. You'll get a thick ear if you're not careful.

Trunch.   Well, there'll be room for that too.

Punch.   How long have you been in the Force ?

Trunch.   I'm a new model.   I haven't been run in yet.

Punch.   *You* don't have to be run in.   You have to run other people in.   Now, look 'ere, Trunch—are you listening ?   (*He lifts up* Trunch's *helmet to see, and puts it back again.*)   We're 'ere to keep the crowd in order.

Trunch.   What, that lot out there ?   (*He points to the audience.*)

Punch.   No—not in front.   Behind you !

(Trunch *swings round, his back to the audience. He can have funny business here, looking for the crowd and not finding it, looking at* Punch *to see if his leg is being pulled, then having another look for the crowd, and so on.*)

Trunch.   Did you say—keep the crowd back ?

Punch (*calmly, staring front*).   That's what I said.

Trunch (*having another look*).   Well—somebody's crackers and I don't think it's me.

Punch.   What's the matter ?

Trunch.   There's no crowd there.

Punch.   There will be, as soon as the Prince arrives.   They'll be swarming around like bees. Now, I'm going to put you on duty here and you've got to keep the crowd in order, see ?   (*He moves towards the house.*)

Trunch.   Where are you going ?

Punch.   I'm—er—just going in 'ere to put my watch right.

Trunch.   When you come out, I'll go in and put mine right.   You're not the only one who's thirsty.

(*Exit* Punch *to the house.   There is cheering off stage.* Villagers *run on from up* L. *and up* R. Trunch *runs about amongst them, shouting :* " Hi !   Stop ! Keep back there, please ! " *etc.   The* Crowd *swarms round the entrance up* L., *and* Trunch, *who has been knocked over two or three times in vain endeavour to control them, is finally confronted with a row of backs, which he tries to push through.   PUNCH rushes out of the house.)*

It's too late, Punch.   They've *swarmed* !

(The CROWD, *cheering and waving, breaks up as the* PRINCE *comes down stage, followed by* DANDY.)

CROWD.   Welcome to Merryvale !

PRINCE.   Thank you, good people, for your welcome. It is *very* encouraging. What say you, Dandy ?

DANDY.   I should describe it as—tumultuous, Your Highness—even overwhelming.

TRUNCH.   Overwhelming is the word !   *(He picks up the helmet which has been knocked off.)*

PRINCE.   Really, I had no idea there were so many pretty faces in Merryvale.   We must come here again, Dandy.   But, first of all, we must pay a visit to the lady of the house.   Now, let me see—what is her name ?

DANDY.   Some name like Rhubarb or Hubbub, I fancy.

PRINCE.   Ah, I remember now.   Wasn't there an old woman who went somewhere to get something for somebody and it was bare or something and so the poor somebody or other didn't get anything ?

DANDY.   Something like that, I believe, sir.

PRINCE.   We must ask the lady.

(They turn towards each other and talk.   MRS. HUB-BARD *bustles out of the house, in a panic at being late.)*

MRS. HUBBARD *(to* TRUNCH, *who is standing down* R. *with* PUNCH). Why didn't you tell me he had arrived !

PUNCH *(pointing to* TRUNCH). He was over-whelmed !

*(*MRS. HUBBARD *begins bowing and curtsying to the* PRINCE, *who has his back to her.   She coughs to*

attract his attention.   The Crowd *try to help matters by coughing too, until everyone is coughing loudly.)*

Prince (*becoming aware of the din*).   Everyone has suddenly got a very bad cough !

Dandy.   I think, sir, your attention is being directed to some performance that is going on behind you.

(*The* Prince *turns and sees* Mrs. Hubbard, *who is still busy bobbing up and down.)*

Prince.   What is it ?   (*Looking at* Mrs. Hubbard *as if she were some queer animal.*)

Dandy.   Dumb charades, I should think, sir.

Mrs. Hubbard.   Hubbard is the name, your Highness.

Prince.   Ah, *you* are Dame Hubbard of the Cupboard !   Now, madam, we are somewhat hungry after our exercise.   We trust the cupboard is not bare to-day.   You can—er—get the poor dog a bone, perhaps ?

Mrs. Hubbard.   Sir, everything is ready.   Tarbel dotty or ahlacarty, whichever you prefer.   (*She holds out the menu.*)

Prince (*handing the menu to* Dandy).   What does it say, Dandy ?

Dandy (*reading*).   Pea soup, fish cakes, cut off joint with two veg. or Lancashire hotpot, syrup roll, cheese, coffee——

Prince (*with a grimace*).   Er—have you a snack bar ?

Mrs. Hubbard.   A—what bar ?

Dandy.   You know—one of those places where you stand up and eat.

Mrs. Hubbard.   The Prince couldn't go *there* !

Prince.   At the snack bar we can stand up and eat, but if we have the—er—tarbel dotty, we shall lie down and die !

(*The* Prince *sees* Red Riding Hood, *who has entered from the house.*)

Who is the little girl in red ?
MRS. HUBBARD.   Oh, she is only my daughter, sir.

(RED RIDING HOOD *curtsys.   The* PRINCE *is lost in admiration.*)

PRINCE.   *Only* your daughter, did you say ?   That is a very casual introduction to one who is—so attractive.   She is shy, is she not ?
MRS. HUBBARD.   She has been a little upset this morning.   She was attacked by a wolf.
PRINCE.   It is disgraceful that the people should be exposed to such dangers on my land.   I must do something about that wolf.   In the meantime—(*he draws* DANDY *on one side*)—will *you* do something about the people.
DANDY (*puzzled*).   The people, sir ?
PRINCE.   Yes.   (*He indicates the* CROWD.)   These people.   Get them away, somehow.   Stand them all ices at my expense.

(*He winks at* DANDY, *who grasps his meaning and winks back.* DANDY *goes to* MRS. HUBBARD *and whispers in her ear.* MRS. HUBBARD *whispers to* PUNCH, *who whispers to* TRUNCH. PUNCH *and* TRUNCH *carry the whispering on into the* CROWD. *Whispering goes on amongst the* CROWD, *who troop off into the house, leaving* RED RIDING HOOD *and the* PRINCE *alone.* RED RIDING HOOD *turns to go too, but the* PRINCE *stops her.*)

No, not you !   I'm not going to stand *you* an ice. I have something warmer to offer.
RED RIDING HOOD.   Something—warmer ?
PRINCE.   Can you guess what it is ?
RED RIDING HOOD.   Soup, perhaps ?
PRINCE (*laughing heartily*).   You are a simple little girl.   Have you never been kissed ?
RED RIDING HOOD.   No, sir.
PRINCE.   Never been kissed ?   The boys must have been very slow round here.
RED RIDING HOOD.   I wouldn't let them kiss me.

Prince. Why not ?

Red Riding Hood. I don't like them—in that way.

Prince. Would you like me—in that way ?

Red Riding Hood (*coyly*). Oh, sir !

(*The* Prince *kisses her.*)

Prince. I didn't wait for your answer. That was rude of me.

Red Riding Hood. I—I—forgive you.

Prince. That makes me bolder. (*He kisses her again.*) I don't think I want any lunch now.

Red Riding Hood. Mother will be very disappointed. Won't you take some light refreshment ?

Prince. *You*—are my light refreshment !

(*Song and dance for the* Prince *and* Red Riding Hood, *which takes them off. The* Witch's *head is seen peering round the wing up* L. *She comes on, chuckling to herself, followed by the* Baron. *They get* C.)

Baron. Now, now, old Witch, what are you doing in the village ?

Witch. I'm up to no good, as usual.

Baron. Your presence here is forbidden. If the Prince sees you it will go hard with you.

Witch. The Prince is too busy, at the moment. He is what you might call—heavily engaged—(*she points off* R. *and cackles at her joke*)—with his little piece of light refreshment—Red Riding Hood !

Baron. Red Riding Hood ? Dame Hubbard's daughter ?

Witch. Yes, and this is where *you* come in.

Baron. I want none of your riddles, old Witch. What's in that ugly head of yours ?

Witch. A scheme, a scheme ! A clever scheme ! There's money in it.

Baron. Ha ! Money, did you say ? Come, what's your scheme ? Out with it.

Witch. Steal the girl and hold her up to ransom.

The Prince will pay. When a man's in love he doesn't count the cost.

BARON. Steal Red Riding Hood ?

WITCH. It's easily done. Twice a week she goes alone through the wood to her grandmother's cottage, with butter and eggs.

BARON. Twice a week ?

WITCH. On Tuesdays and Fridays.

BARON (*reflecting*). It can't be done. (*Put in a local gag here.*) Couldn't she make it Mondays and Thursdays ?

WITCH. It can be arranged——

BARON. Then let us lay our plans.

(*The* BARON *and* WITCH *go off* L.
    Enter up R. SIMPLE SIMON, *wheeling an ice-cream barrow, followed by* GIRLS *from the chorus.*)

GIRLS. How much are the ices, Simon ?

SIMPLE SIMON. There's no charge, young ladies. They're free to-day. Prince's orders are that every-one is to have an ice. I'm going to give you a large ice-cream cornet each so you can all have a good licking !

(*Laughter.*)

(*As he speaks, and during the introductory bars of the song, he serves out the cornets. Cotton-wool can be used to represent ice-cream.*)

(*Song by* SIMPLE SIMON.)

(*The following verse and chorus can easily be set to music. The words of the chorus should be lowered on a sheet and* SIMPLE SIMON *should get the audience to sing them in the traditional manner.*)

Verse.

Simple Simon met a pieman, going to the Fair.
Said Simple Simon to the pieman, " What have you
    got there ? "

The pieman said, "I don't sell pies, my ices brought
　　me fame."
Then Simon said, "Well, ice ain't nice, but I'll have
　　one just the same."

Chorus.

Why do I like a nice ice-cream,
'Cos a nice ice-cream's not nice ?
It makes your mouth go oh so numb,
And it gives you a pain in the tummy-tum-tum.
If you make it hot, you lose the lot,
For it has to be as cold as ice, SO !
Why do I like a nice ice-cream ?
Well, a nice ice-cream's so nice !

(SIMPLE SIMON *is about to wheel his barrow off, when he
stops and listens.*)

What was that ? I heard a scream.
　GIRLS. A scream ?
　SIMPLE SIMON. Yes. Not a (n)ice (s)cream either.

(*A* GIRL'S *scream is heard off.*)

There it is again !

(*The* GIRL *runs on up* L., *screaming,* " The Wolf !
The Wolf ! " *The* CHORUS *panic.* KING WOLF
appears up L. SIMPLE SIMON *leaps in the air with
fright and runs into the house, leaving his barrow
behind.* KING WOLF *chases the* CHORUS *off* R. *and*
L., *returns to* C., *helps himself to a large ice-cream
cornet and creeps off up* L., *licking the ice.* PUNCH
and TRUNCH *enter hurriedly* R.)

　TRUNCH. Which way did he go ?
　PUNCH. How do I know. Look for the spoor.
　TRUNCH. Look for the—what ?
　PUNCH. Spoor ! Don't you know what a spoor
is ?
　TRUNCH. All right, I'll buy it.
　PUNCH. You don't have to buy it, you have to
look for it. Come on.

(PUNCH *starts to look on the ground for tracks of the* WOLF, *and* TRUNCH, *after watching him for a moment, starts looking too, until eventually they crash their heads together.*)

TRUNCH.   I've seen 'em !
PUNCH.   The spoor ?
TRUNCH.   No, the stars.   (*He counts stars in dazed fashion.*)
PUNCH.   Here are the wolf's tracks.   (*He follows the tracks round.   They lead up to the ice-cream barrow.*) Blimey !   He's been at the ice-cream !

(*Enter the* PRINCE, *followed by* DANDY *and* MRS. HUBBARD, *from the house.*)

PRINCE.   Summon the villagers at once !

(*Exit* DANDY *up* L.)

This wolf must be hunted down and killed.
TRUNCH.   He's been at the ice-cream.
MRS. HUBBARD.   Did he leave any money ?
TRUNCH.   No.
MRS. HUBBARD.   He's a dirty dog !

(*The* VILLAGERS *enter and the* PRINCE *addresses them.*)

PRINCE.   Men and women of Merryvale, you must be brave.   You are not *sheep* that you can be *foxed* by the *monkey*-tricks of this *wolf*.   You must *ferret* him out, *hound* him from the wood and shoot him like a *dog*.   It may prove to be an *elephantine* task, but you will succeed if you are *lion*-hearted, and if that isn't good *horse*-sense, you can write me down an *ass* !   I offer five hundred pounds for the body of King Wolf—alive or dead—dead for preference. So now—all of you—to your task !

(*The* CROWD *cheers the* PRINCE *as he exits up* L.)

Tableau for CURTAIN.

ACT II

SCENE 1

The wood.   This scene can be played on half-stage, so that Scene 2 may be partially set up behind to avoid a long wait.   A large notice, " Trespassers will be Prosecuted," is displayed on the " drop."   There is a log-seat down L.

The CURTAIN *rises on a number of* HIKERS *sitting around, having halted here for lunch.   Thermos-flasks, sandwich packets, etc., are scattered about.   There is an opportunity here for some community singing, or a scouts' " sing-song."*

Enter GAMEKEEPER WOOD, *a rather bovine character. The sort of man to whom " orders is orders."   He carries a gun and, to make his entrance funnier, he can be followed by a dog on wheels.*

GAMEKEEPER.   I suppose you young ladies and gentlemen know you're trespassing.

1ST HIKER.   Oh, you *do* use long words !

GAMEKEEPER.   Well, if the word ain't familiar, it's there—in black and white. (*He points to the notice.*)

2ND HIKER.   Talking of Black and White—would you like a drink ?   (*He holds up a bottle of whisky.*)

GAMEKEEPER.   I don't want no drink.

3RD HIKER.   He's used the double negative ! An *uneducated* gamekeeper !

GAMEKEEPER.   Now look 'ere, you young ladies and gentlemen——

HIKERS (*interrupting*).   Do you know you're tres-

30

passing ? No, we don't. We're awfully sorry, Mr. Gamekeeper.

1st HIKER. We're not doing any harm.

GAMEKEEPER. Ah, that's what they *all* says.

1st HIKER (*to the* HIKERS). *There*, you see. I've said the right thing !

GAMEKEEPER. You're disturbing the game.

2ND HIKER. You're disturbing the show !

GAMEKEEPER. How did you get here ?

1st HIKER. It's all in the Ramblers' Guide.

GAMEKEEPER. Oh, is it ? Then there must be some mistake. This is the Baron's private property.

1st HIKER. There's no mistake. (*He produces a book.*) If you are not familiar with the route, it's here—in black and white.

(*Laughter from the* HIKERS. *The* 1st HIKER *reads from the book.*)

"—After leaving Merryvale Station, turn left at Ye Olde Cupboarde Inn, follow road for two miles, turn right into cart-track, cross field of stubble by footpath, enter wood——"

GAMEKEEPER (*interrupting*). Ah ! Enter *Wood* ! That's where I come in, you see.

1st HIKER. We don't see.

GAMEKEEPER. Well, my name's Wood, you see.

2ND HIKER. Oh—*I* see. You're *Wood* and you've just come on. Enter Wood—that's rather good.

(*They all laugh.*)

3RD HIKER. It rhymes, too.

1st HIKER. Why, of course, it's a stage direction. Enter Wood.

2ND HIKER (*standing up*). Enter Wood—exeunt Hikers !

GAMEKEEPER. And the sooner, the better.

1st HIKER (*rising*). Well, of course, we don't want to hold up the show, do we, boys and girls ?

(*The* HIKERS *all rise as the music of a marching song
strikes up. They march off to the music, the last
one to leave detaching the notice " Trespassers will
be Prosecuted " and hanging it on the barrel of the*
GAMEKEEPER'S *gun. The* GAMEKEEPER *hangs it up
again. As he is doing this a "* SWEET YOUNG
THING *" in hiking costume enters* L. *and goes to him* C.)

SWEET YOUNG THING. Can you tell me please
—am I all right for Chorley Wood ?

GAMEKEEPER (*embarrassed by her charms*). Well
—I don't rightly know.

SWEET YOUNG THING. You don't know ? Are
you a stranger ?

GAMEKEEPER. Well, I am—to *you*, missy.

SWEET YOUNG THING. That doesn't matter. I
only want to know if I'm all right for Chorley Wood.

GAMEKEEPER (*shyly*). Well, you see, missy—I'm
Charlie Wood ! (*He pronounces it " Chawlie."*)

SWEET YOUNG THING (*puzzled*). You are—Chorley
Wood !

GAMEKEEPER. That's my name, missy.

SWEET YOUNG THING. That's your—— Oh, I *see*.

(*She begins to laugh as the mistake dawns on her, then,
overcome by the absurd situation, she bursts into
uncontrolled laughter. She becomes so weak from
laughing that she droops helplessly and perilously
over the end of the* GAMEKEEPER'S *gun, which he
hastily points the other way. She recovers, goes to
the exit* R., *turns, gives him one more look, bursts
into another fit of laughter, and exits.*)

GAMEKEEPER (*staring after her with a puzzled
expression*). There's something funny about me,
but I'm durned if I know what 'tis.

(*Song by the* GAMEKEEPER.)

(*Enter the* BARON, L.)

BARON. Anything to report, Gamekeeper Wood ?

GAMEKEEPER. Just 'ad a party of trespassers, sir.

But they soon skedaddled when I came in.   (*Proudly.*)
—Enter Wood, exit Hikers. It's all down in black
and white.

BARON (*suspiciously*). You haven't had any, have
you ?

GAMEKEEPER. Any what ?

BARON. Black and White.

GAMEKEEPER. Not yet, sir, but I'm livin' in
'opes.

BARON. You shall have some if you do a special
job for me.

GAMEKEEPER. A special job ?

BARON. Yes. I want you to do a little—er—
business of abduction.

GAMEKEEPER. Abduction ! If that there's arith-
metic, I'm no good at figures.

BARON (*darkly*). There's only one figure in this
and you've got to abduct it.

GAMEKEEPER (*suspiciously*). You haven't 'ad any,
'ave you ?

BARON. Any what ?

GAMEKEEPER. Black and White.

BARON. Listen. I'm looking for a little girl in a
red cloak, a red hood, and carrying a basket.

(*The* GAMEKEEPER'S *face lights up.*)

GAMEKEEPER. A little girl ?

BARON (*excitedly*). Yes ! Have you seen her ?

GAMEKEEPER (*eagerly*). A little girl, wearing a red
cloak—— ?

BARON. Yes !

GAMEKEEPER. A red hood ?

BARON. Yes !

GAMEKEEPER. And carrying a basket ?

BARON (*beside himself with excitement*). Yes, yes !

GAMEKEEPER (*disappointedly*). No, I haven't seen
her. (*He looks sadly off* R.) It must have been
another little girl. She asked me if she was " all
right for me," and she *was* all right for me, all right,
but she ran away.

BARON. This girl is known as Little Red Riding Hood. If you see her, you are to carry her off immediately to Grandmother Hubbard's cottage.

GAMEKEEPER. But what will the old lady think of such goings on ?

BARON. She won't be there. I'll see to that. (*With sinister meaning.*)

GAMEKEEPER. But supposin' the little girl *won't* be carried off ?

BARON. You must use force.

GAMEKEEPER (*astonished*). Use force ?

BARON. Arrest her for trespassing on my land.

GAMEKEEPER. Ah, now I understand, sir. Trespassers will be prosecuted. It's down in black and white. (*He points to the notice.*)

BARON. You'll want some help. Go and get your assistant, and hurry up or you may miss the girl.

GAMEKEEPER. Very good, sir.

(*He exits* R.)

BARON. And now to the cottage—to deal with Grandmother Hubbard.

(*He exits* R.   *Enter* L., MRS. HUBBARD, *in riding-habit.*)

MRS. HUBBARD (*addressing the audience*). Well, girls, how d'you like my habit ? Is it a good habit or is it a bad habit ? I'm taking up equitation, as you see. All young girls go in for riding nowadays. There's nothing like equestrian exercise for developing one's—well, one's business. Take my business. If I put up a notice outside my inn, " Halt ! Hubbard's Hacks for Hire ! Good Pull-up for Hikers," I shall make a small fortune—or a large funeral.

(*There is opportunity here for a song number by* MRS. HUBBARD. *Also, after the song, there is an opening for a pantomime horse, brought on by* SIMPLE SIMON. *Funny business with the horse can be worked up until the arrival of* PUNCH *and* TRUNCH. *If the horse is not practicable, the book can be continued, as follows.*)

(*Enter* SIMPLE SIMON, *after the song.*)

Now, Simon, where's the horse ?

SIMPLE SIMON. Sorry, Mother. They can't let you have one to-day.

MRS. HUBBARD. Why not ?

SIMPLE SIMON. They say there isn't one available.

MRS. HUBBARD. What about the chestnut ?

SIMPLE SIMON. They say it's getting too old.

MRS. HUBBARD. Well—there's the grey mare.

SIMPLE SIMON. She's got galloping consumption.

MRS. HUBBARD. What about the bay gelding ?

SIMPLE SIMON. That's too fresh for you.

MRS. HUBBARD. I don't want a *stale* one ! It looks to me as if they don't want me to have a horse at all. Come with me, Simon. I shall go and see for myself.

(*She exits* R.)

SIMPLE SIMON (*lagging behind*). And when she got there, the stable was bare—and so the old girl had none !

(*He exits* R.   *Enter* PUNCH *and* TRUNCH, L.)

PUNCH. Now, Trunch, you know what we're 'ere for, don't you ?

TRUNCH. No, I don't !

PUNCH. You don't ? You're a nice policeman !

TRUNCH. Kiss me, Sergeant ! (*He repeats business as in Act I.*)

PUNCH. Listen, Trunch. We're going to lure the wolf into a trap, and you've got to be the decoy !

TRUNCH. De—wot ?

PUNCH. Decoy. You've heard of a decoy duck, 'aven't you ? Well, you're going to be the decoy wolf.

TRUNCH. What do I have to do ?

PUNCH (*undoing the bundle which he has brought on*). You have to put on this cloak and hood, so that you'll look like little Red Riding Hood.

TRUNCH. Do I look like little Red Riding Hood ?

PUNCH. No, you don't. You're much too beautiful. But if you pull the hood well down over your
face, the wolf won't know the difference. (*He has
put the cloak on* TRUNCH *and pulls the hood down over
his face.*) Don't you see what I mean ?

TRUNCH. Not under this.

PUNCH (*adjusting the hood*). Now, as soon as the
wolf sees you, of course, he'll want to attack you.

TRUNCH. Oh, he will *want* to attack me, will he ?

PUNCH. Yes, because he thinks you're little Red
Riding Hood, see ? Well, as soon as you catch sight
of him, you whip out your whistle and you give three
blasts.

TRUNCH. Three blasts ! Not three cheers ?

PUNCH. Then I rush out of my ambush——

TRUNCH. I was wondering when *you* were coming
in——

PUNCH. —with my men——

TRUNCH. *Your* men ! Don't *I* have any men ?

PUNCH —and catch him in the rear.

TRUNCH. And—what do *I* do ?

PUNCH. You catch him in the front.

TRUNCH. With *my* men.

PUNCH. No, you don't have any men. *I* have
the men.

TRUNCH (*taking off the cloak*). *You* can be Red
Riding Hood !

PUNCH. Don't be silly. I'm much too big.
(*He gives the cloak back.*) Come on, Trunch. Be a
man !

TRUNCH. Oh, I've got to be a man, now, have I ?

PUNCH. Think of that five hundred pounds
reward !

TRUNCH. How much do I get ?

PUNCH. You'll get the lion's share.

TRUNCH. Oh, there's a lion in it too, is there ?
Any tigers as well ?—because, I mean to say, we
may as well 'ave a bit o' fun while we're about it.

PUNCH. Don't you worry. It'll work out all

right.   Now, you sit down there, like a good little
girl—— (*He pushes* TRUNCH *on to the log-seat.*)
   TRUNCH.   Kiss me, Sergeant !
   PUNCH.   Have you got your whistle ?
   TRUNCH (*meekly*).   Yes, Sergeant.
   PUNCH (*going off* R.).   Don't forget—three blasts !
   TRUNCH.   And the same to you !

(*Exit* PUNCH R.   TRUNCH *pulls out his whistle and
   tries it to see if it is in order.   It is stopped up and
   while he is endeavouring to get some sound out of it,
   the* FAIRY QUEEN *enters* R.   *She sees what appears
   to be* RED RIDING HOOD *crying convulsively and goes
   up to comfort her, in the traditional manner.*)

   FAIRY QUEEN.   Little Red Riding Hood, don't sob
      so much.
See, I will calm you, with my magic touch !

(*She touches him with her wand.   He pulls his hood
   down over his face and turns his back on her.*)

(*Aside.*)   She does not recognize her Fairy Queen.
This is too awful.   It will ruin my scene !

(She tries again.)

Little Red Riding Hood, you must not cry.
No harm can come to you while I am nigh !

(*There is no response.   The* FAIRY QUEEN *goes
          bravely on.*)

Though nought can harm you while you're in the wood,
It's time you moved on—Little Red Riding Hood.
(*Aside.*)   Still she is dumb, with not a word to say.
I only have just one more card to play !
I'd better play it now. (*She turns to* TRUNCH.)
      Take this gold brooch.
It will protect you from the wolf's approach.

(*As she hands the brooch,* TRUNCH, *still under his hood,
          shoots out a hand and snatches it.*)

At any rate, she seems to know *that* cue.

She snatches, though, as if it were her due
Instead of my free gift. But come what may,
I've done my duty, now I must away.

(*Exit the* Fairy Queen, l. Trunch *emerges from
his hood.*)

Trunch. Well, as something's gone wrong with
my whistle, I'd better put on her brooch.

(*As he is occupied with pinning on the brooch,* Gamekeeper Wood *creeps on* r., *followed by* Splinter,
a small assistant.)

Gamekeeper (*whispering*). There she is ! Red
hood, red cloak, and basket. It's the girl all right.
Hold my gun ! (*He gives the gun to* Splinter.)
Now, stand by in case she struggles.

(*The* Gamekeeper *creeps up behind* Trunch, *and with
a quick movement ties a gag over his mouth.* Trunch
struggles, but the Gamekeeper *picks him up and
carries him off* l., *followed by* Splinter *with the
gun and the basket.
The* Witch *runs on* r., *chuckling with glee.*)

Witch. I've made it awkward for that Fairy
Queen !
She's got things muddled up as you have seen.
She only has one brooch, so there's no doubt
The real Red Riding Hood must go without.
The truth will out in Grandma Hubbard's cottage,
And then they'll all be deeply in the pottage !

(*She runs off* l.)

(*To provide a good* Curtain, *dim the lights, and bring
on* King Wolf *to suitable music. He is seen
creeping slowly across the stage from* r. *to* l., *followed, after his exit, at a short interval, by* Red
Riding Hood, *carrying her basket, as if on her way
to the cottage.*)

Curtain.

SCENE 2

GRANDMA HUBBARD'S *cottage.   Interior.   There is a
door back* C., *another door down* L., *a bed up* L. *and
a dressing-table and looking-glass* R.

The CURTAIN *rises on an empty stage.   The door back*
C. *opens slowly and* KING WOLF *looks in.   He creeps
to the bed, looks on it and underneath it, scratches
his head in perplexity, then, catching sight of the door
down* L., *creeps to it and knocks gently.* GRANDMA
HUBBARD'S *voice is heard calling, "* Come in.*"*
KING WOLF *registers gleeful satisfaction.   He opens
the door and creeps through, shutting the door behind
him.* GRANDMA'S *voice is heard shrieking and
calling for help.   There is the sound of commotion,
furniture being knocked over, etc., then silence.*

During the pause, the door back C. *opens again
and the* BARON *enters.   He repeats* KING WOLF'S
business of looking for GRANDMA HUBBARD *and is
on his way to the door down* L. *when his move is
arrested by loud knocking on the door back* C.
SPLINTER *puts his head through.*

SPLINTER.   Anybody at home ?
BARON (*startled*).   Who is that ?
SPLINTER.   I don't know.   I'll ask.   (*He with-
draws his head.*)

(*The* BARON *goes to the door back* C. *and flings it open,
discovering* SPLINTER *with the gun and the basket.*
SPLINTER *walks in.*)

I've found out who it is.   It's me !
BARON.   Where is Gamekeeper Wood ?
SPLINTER.   Coming   along.   He's   caught   a
trespasser.
BARON.   Ah !—wearing a red cloak ?
SPLINTER.   Yes.
BARON.   Carrying a basket ?
SPLINTER.   Yes.   Here's the basket.
BARON (*seizing the basket*).   He's got the girl !
SPLINTER.   Some girl !

BARON. What ?

SPLINTER. That girl's got a few tricks she didn't learn at a girls' school. She struggled so much, she hit her napper against a tree-trunk and now she's unconscious.

(*Enter the* GAMEKEEPER, *carrying* TRUNCH, *still with gag.*)

GAMEKEEPER. Here you are, sir. I 'ope it's all right.

BARON. Put her on the bed. (*He rubs his hands with satisfaction.*)

(*The* GAMEKEEPER *puts* TRUNCH *on the bed so that his feet hang over the edge in full view of the audience.*)

SPLINTER. She's got nice, dainty little feet, 'asn't she !

GAMEKEEPER (*surprised*). They look to me like the feet of Police-Constable Trunch.

(*The* BARON *lifts up the cloak.*)

SPLINTER. There's some more of Police-Constable Trunch farther up.

(*The* BARON *pulls the cloak right off.*)

GAMEKEEPER (*amazed*). Why, it's Constable Trunch himself ! (*He removes the gag.*)

BARON (*facing front*). There are some other plots afoot. That old hag has played me false !

GAMEKEEPER. If I hadn't put that gag on I should have known who it was by the voice. Splinter— we've assaulted the force. We've been and gone and *done* it.

SPLINTER (*to the* BARON). You'd better tell the constable we've been and gone and—never come !

(*Exit hurriedly* SPLINTER *and the* GAMEKEEPER. *The* BARON *takes the cloak and the basket.*)

BARON. I'd better hide these. They might be used as evidence against me.

(*He crosses to the door* L.   TRUNCH *comes to, suddenly,
and sits up.*)

TRUNCH.   Hi!

(*The* BARON *turns in a great fright.*)

Where am I ?
BARON (*uncertainly*).   You—er—you're in bed.
TRUNCH (*suspiciously*).   Who's bed ?
BARON.   Grandma Hubbard's bed.

(*The* BARON *tries to hide the cloak and basket behind him.*)

TRUNCH.   What am I doin' in Grandma Hubbard's
bed ?   (*Getting up and rubbing his head.*)
BARON.   It's no good asking me.   I've got nothing
to do with it.
TRUNCH (*still rather dazed*).   Excuse me, miss, but
your petticoat's coming down.
BARON.   It's all right.   (*He shows more of the cloak
in his agitation.*)
TRUNCH (*jumping off the bed*).   Let me help you !
(*He catches hold of the cloak.*)   Where did you get this ?
BARON (*holding on and shouting*).   Mind your own
business !
TRUNCH.   Blimey !   Are you trying to be Little
Red Riding Hood too !   Ah !   I remember !   It's all
coming back to me.
BARON.   What is ?
TRUNCH.   This is !   (*He snatches the cloak from
the* BARON.)   I've been kidnapped !

(*The* BARON *snatches the cloak back.   They struggle.
Enter* PUNCH, *back* C.)

PUNCH.   You're a *nice* policeman !

(TRUNCH *drops the cloak and runs to* PUNCH.)

TRUNCH.   Kiss me, Sergeant !
PUNCH.   Now then—none o' that.
BARON.   Sergeant, your assistant here is a fool.
He's not fit to wear the uniform.
PUNCH (*scornfully*).   His uniform ain't fit to wear !

Baron. Is that why he has to wear woman's clothes ?

Punch. That's just a trap, sir. A decoy, sir. Clever bit o' sleuthin' on the part of the Merryvale Constabulary. (*He winks at* Trunch.) Set a sprat to catch a mackerel !

Trunch. Who are you callin' a sprat !

Punch. We seem to have missed the mackerel, but we've caught something else. I'm going to get promotion out of this, or my name ain't Sergeant Punch. And you, Trunch—I shouldn't be surprised if you got a stripe.

Baron (*angry*). He'll get a stripe where he doesn't expect it—and more than one !

Punch. Just a moment, sir. I hear as how you're mixed up in this plot.

Baron. What plot ?

Punch. This 'ere plot to kidnap Red Riding Hood, the Prince's sweetheart. Gamekeeper Charlie 'as been spillin' the beans !

Baron (*raging*). I'll spill his beans !

Punch. Then you *do* know something about it ! I'm afraid I'll have to detain you, sir !

(Punch *takes out his notebook and pencil.*)

D'you mind giving me a few particulars ?

(*While* Punch *is busy finding a place in his notebook, the* Baron *makes a quick movement and bolts through the door back* c. *When* Punch *looks up the* Baron *has disappeared.*)

Where's he gone ?

Trunch (*who has been occupied with the cloak, etc.*). I dunno !

Punch (*killing him with a look*). You're a *nice policeman* !

(Punch *darts out through the door in pursuit of the* Baron.)

Trunch. Wait for me, Sergeant !

(*He follows* PUNCH, *leaving the cloak behind.   The*
WITCH *appears at the doorway back* C.   *She laughs*
as she watches the chase and then enters and
comes C.)

WITCH.   My scheme is working well, see how they
    run.
There's only one thing more, now, to be done.
The magic brooch ! the magic brooch ! It's here !
    (*She seizes the cloak.*)
I'll take it off now, while the coast is clear. (*She*
    unpins the brooch.)
And now it's done—well, I don't want to boast,
But I shall have that Fairy Queen on toast !

(*Enter the* FAIRY QUEEN, *back* C.)

FAIRY QUEEN.   Well, here she is !
WITCH (*in triumph*).   Too late ! Too late !
FAIRY QUEEN.   Not too late to hear your boasting.
So I'm to be on toast now, am I ? The last time
we met I was to be put in the soup. You don't
seem to know what you want, old Witch.
WITCH.   I know what I want. I have always
known what I want. Revenge ! And now my hour
has come. You have made a mistake at last. You
have parted with your magic. See, I have the
brooch. (*She holds up the brooch.*) Your power is
gone. Like the bee which leaves its sting behind,
you will die !
FAIRY QUEEN (*not at all put out*). If I am to be
a bee—I must beehive myself. To be a bee or not
to be—that is the question.
WITCH.   Joking won't help you now. You gave
your token to Red Riding Hood—but not to the real
Red Riding Hood. (*She chuckles.*)
FAIRY QUEEN (*slyly*). And—not the real token,
perhaps.

(*The* WITCH *glares at the* FAIRY QUEEN *and then looks*
    anxiously at the brooch.   The FAIRY QUEEN *holds*
    out another brooch.)

As you see, old Witch, there are two. The one you have is only imitation.

(There is a howl of rage from the WITCH.)

I saw through your little plans and laid mine accordingly. You should remember that the bad fairy can never win—in the end—and she who laughs last, laughs loudest.

(Exit the FAIRY QUEEN, *back* O., *laughing. The* WITCH *runs to the doorway and shakes her fist.)*

WITCH. You have outwitted me this time, but I can wait. My time will come. Beauty will fade! Beauty will fade! And the old witch will come into her own!

(The WITCH *disappears through the doorway back* O.

KING WOLF *returns through the door down* L., *carrying* GRANDMA HUBBARD'S *nightgown and cap. He now has the stage to himself and can work up business of retiring to bed. First, he shuts the door back* O. *Then he puts the nightgown round him so that it can easily be slipped off, and sits down at the dressing-table. Laughs can be got by having the usual toilet bottles and hairbrushes, etc., on the table, which he can use. It is a good idea to have no glass in the mirror so that he drops things on the wrong side and pushes his paws through the mirror-frame to recover them. When he has cleaned his teeth, he puts on a nightcap, gets into bed, switches on the bedside lamp, or lights a candle, picks up a newspaper and pretends to read.*

RED RIDING HOOD *arrives at the door back* O., *knocks, and calls "*Grandma!*"* KING WOLF *hurriedly puts down the paper, extinguishes the light, and lies down.)*

KING WOLF *(imitating* GRANDMA). Lift the latch, my dear, and come in!

(Enter RED RIDING HOOD.)

RED RIDING HOOD. Are you in bed, Grandma ?
KING WOLF. Yes, my dear. Come right up beside me. Don't be afraid. I haven't got the flu !

(RED RIDING HOOD *goes to the bedside.*)

RED RIDING HOOD. Why, Grandma, how big your eyes are !
KING WOLF. All the better to see you with, my dear.
RED RIDING HOOD. And how big your ears have grown !
KING WOLF. All the better to hear you with !
RED RIDING HOOD. And what great big teeth you've got !
KING WOLF. All the better *to eat you with !*

(KING WOLF *pulls off his cap and springs out of bed. RED RIDING HOOD screams and runs down* R. *KING WOLF runs after her. As they struggle, the* PRINCE *enters quickly back* C., *sword in hand. He makes a pass at* KING WOLF, *who falls.* RED RIDING HOOD *subsides into the* PRINCE'S *arms.* DANDY *enters back* C., *very much out of breath.*)

DANDY. Am I too late, sir ?
PRINCE. Yes, Dandy—too late to win a medal. But you can—er—view the body.
DANDY. Is he dead ?
PRINCE. Well, you'd better make sure. I'm busy.

(DANDY *kneels over* KING WOLF.)

RED RIDING HOOD. You have saved my life ! Oh, my Prince !
PRINCE. Did you say—" *my* prince " ?
RED RIDING HOOD. Yes, I—I'm afraid I did.
PRINCE. Don't be afraid, my pretty one. For when *you* say " my Prince," *I* can say " my Princess." (*He kisses her.*)
DANDY. King Wolf is dead !

(*The* PRINCE *and* RED RIDING HOOD *are too occupied to heed him.*)

And—if I may say so—we arrived just in time!
PRINCE (*turning to him and smiling*). Yes—what a good thing it was we—er—happened to be passing!

(*The* PRINCE *and* RED RIDING HOOD *embrace.* DANDY, *embarrassed, looks the other way.*)

The CURTAIN *falls.*

ACT III

SCENE.—*The* PRINCE'S *Palace.   Interior.*
  There is an archway back C., *providing entrances* R. *and* L. *down two or three steps, and upper and lower side entrances.*

The CHORUS, *representing the guests of the* PRINCE, *are engaged in a lively dance as the* CURTAIN *rises. A* FOOTMAN *appears in the archway and announces :*

FOOTMAN.   His Royal Highness Prince Charming !

(*Fanfare.   Enter* PRINCE CHARMING, *back* C., *followed by* DANDY.   *They pass down* C. *between the* GUESTS, *who dress the stage* R. *and* L.)

PRINCE.   Welcome, good people, to my humble abode.

(*Cheers from the* CHORUS.)

(*Aside to* DANDY.) Have I said the right thing, Dandy ?

DANDY (*bowing in agreement*).   " Humble abode " is good, your Highness. Very—er—matey, if I may be allowed to use the epithet.

PRINCE.   Good. I want to make them feel at home.

DANDY.   I don't think you'll find they want any encouragement.

PRINCE.   They are certainly very energetic. They have been flinging their arms and legs about in the most abandoned fashion.

DANDY.   Sheer animal spirits, sire.

PRINCE.   I hope it *is* only *animal* spirits.

DANDY.   Animal spirits which must be attributed to the success of the National Fitness Campaign of which you are an ardent patron.

PRINCE.   Judging by their antics just now, there does not seem to be much difference between the fitness of the nation and the nation having a fit.

DANDY.   They are so keen that if you told them to stand on their heads they wouldn't hesitate to do so.

PRINCE.   That might be an improvement, but I think we had better keep them the right way up. They are easier to get rid of that way.

DANDY.   Does your Highness wish to be alone ?

PRINCE (*nodding*).   I am sure they must have developed a thirst.   Announce that there will be an interval for refreshments.

DANDY.   There is a running buffet.

PRINCE.   Then tell them where it is.

(DANDY *turns and addresses the* CHORUS.)

DANDY.   This way out, ladies and gentlemen, for refreshments.   The running buffet is on your right. No—not you, sir !   (*This is said to a member of the audience who, by prearrangement, rises to include himself in the invitation.*)

(*The* GUESTS *run off excitedly up* R.)

PRINCE.   They are very thirsty.   See how they run !

DANDY.   It's just their ignorance, sir.   They've never heard of a *running* buffet before.   They are trying to catch it up.

PRINCE.   That will help the National Fitness Campaign.   Now, I wish to talk of—er—affairs of state.

DANDY.   Affairs of state ?

PRINCE.   Yes—*my* state.

DANDY (*puzzled*).   *Your* state ?

PRINCE.   Yes.   I'm in an awful state !

DANDY.   I'm sorry to hear that, sir.

PRINCE.   Feel my pulse.

DANDY (*feeling his pulse*). Yes—it's doing over thirty. Your Highness must be in the decontrolled area.

PRINCE.   I certainly am !

DANDY.   Have you been off your food lately ?

PRINCE.   Can't touch it !

DANDY.   Sleeping badly ?

PRINCE.   Not a wink.

DANDY.   I think—er—I think I can guess who the young lady is, your Highness.

PRINCE.   Do you know anything about first aid ?

DANDY.   I have been through a course, of course.

PRINCE.   Then it is your duty to prevent the patient from getting worse.

DANDY.   I think, sir, in view of the nature of your ailment, you must get worse—in order to get better.

PRINCE.   Get worse ! You mean that I must ask her to marry me—and risk her saying " No."

DANDY.   What about indirect action ?   You could consult her mother first, to see how the land lies.

PRINCE.   Too difficult.

DANDY.   Not at all, sir. She and her family are your guests to-night.

PRINCE.   What is the best way to approach her on this delicate matter ?

DANDY.   I should advise putting her at her ease, at first, by a show of flattery. The ladies like it, you know.

PRINCE (*reflecting*).   I will take your advice, Dandy. I will go away now and prepare myself for the ordeal, and leave you in charge of the festivities.

(*Exit the* PRINCE *down* R.   DANDY *walks* R.

    Enter through the archway back C., MRS. HUBBARD, RED RIDING HOOD *and* SIMPLE SIMON.   SIMON *has a tin of sweets.* MRS. HUBBARD *is extravagantly dressed. She studies the* FOOTMAN, *who is staring front with haughty expression.*)

MRS. HUBBARD.   Is this the palace or the wax-works ?

SIMPLE SIMON (*to the* FOOTMAN).   Have an 'umbug ?
(*He offers him sweets.*)
FOOTMAN (*in loud and deep tones*).   Name, please ?
MRS. HUBBARD.   Just say "Mrs. Hubbard and family."
FOOTMAN (*bending down*).   Mrs. Who ?
MRS. HUBBARD.   Hubbard, you fool !
FOOTMAN (*announcing*).   Mrs. Hubbardjerfool !
(*he gives the others a contemptuous look*)—and family.

(MRS. HUBBARD *advances down the steps to* DANDY.
She trips over her dress.)

MRS. HUBBARD.   Is this the right day ?
DANDY (*bowing*).   Madam has made no mistake.
MRS. HUBBARD.   Thank goodness !   It would have been just too terrible to arrive on the *wrong* day—especially in this dress.   It took me all day to get into it.   I shall want a week to get out.   Oh, by the way, this is my daughter.   You've met before, I think.   And this, I regret to say, is my son !
SIMPLE SIMON (*offering the sweets*).   Have an 'umbug ?
MRS. HUBBARD.   He's known for his simplicity —which is rather surprising, considering how subtle his mother is.

(*While* DANDY *is shaking hands, she walks round and surveys the scenery through her lorgnettes.*)

MRS. HUBBARD.   Nice little place you've got here !
RED RIDING HOOD (*with excitement*).   I suppose we're in the Grand Ballroom !
DANDY (*off-handedly*).   Oh no, this is just one of the smaller reception rooms.
RED RIDING HOOD.   How disappointing !
DANDY.   The ballroom is in the main building.
MRS. HUBBARD (*feeling slighted*).   Aren't *we* in the main building ?
DANDY.   No, madam.   This is only the annexe.
MRS. HUBBARD (*annoyed*).   So we've been *annexed*, have *we* ?

RED RIDING HOOD (*pointing* R.).   Where does that lead to ?

DANDY.   The guests' quarters.

RED RIDING HOOD (*points up* L.).   And there ?

DANDY.   The servants' quarters.

RED RIDING HOOD (*points down* L.).   And through there ?

DANDY.   The grooms' quarters.

MRS. HUBBARD.   Quarters to the left of us, quarters to the right of us—nothing but *quarters.*

DANDY.   The Prince was never one to do things by *halves*, madam.

(SIMPLE SIMON *goes into a fit of laughter.*)

MRS. HUBBARD (*sternly*).   What are you laughing at, Simon ?

SIMPLE SIMON.   I was just wondering (*pointing to the* FOOTMAN)—where are the hall porter's quarters ?

(*Exit the* FOOTMAN, *annoyed.*)

DANDY.   I think the Prince wishes to see you, madam—privately.

MRS. HUBBARD.   Privately ?

DANDY.   So he said, madam.

MRS. HUBBARD (*gratified*).   Where ?

SIMPLE SIMON.   In the Prince's quarters !

MRS. HUBBARD.   Simon, behave yourself. Remember where you are.

SIMPLE SIMON.   I'm in the guests' quarters—sitting on my hind quarters ! (*He sits on chair and goes into another fit of laughter.*)

DANDY.   I will tell the Prince that you have arrived, madam.

(*Exit* DANDY, R.   MRS. HUBBARD *stares front with a wistful expression.*)

MRS. HUBBARD.   He wants to see me—alone ! That can only mean one thing.

RED RIDING HOOD.   What, Mother ?

Mrs. Hubbard (*still staring front*).   He's fallen for me !

Red Riding Hood.   But, Mother——

Mrs. Hubbard.   How blind I've been not to notice it before !

Red Riding Hood.   But, Mother, listen——

Mrs. Hubbard (*taking no notice*).   That's why he came to lunch the other day.

Red Riding Hood.   Mother, you don't understand——

Mrs. Hubbard (*now completely carried away*). And there was I—bowing and scraping to him, when I should have been casting alluring glances——

Red Riding Hood.   Mother, please listen——

Mrs. Hubbard.   Vamping myself to victory !

(*This ecstatic business can be worked up ad lib. until* Dandy's *entrance down* r.)

Dandy.   Madam, the Prince awaits you without.

Mrs. Hubbard.   Without !   He shall not be *without* for long.   My hour has come !

Dandy.   It won't take as long as that.   Follow me, madam.

(Dandy *leads the way off* r.)

Mrs. Hubbard (*following him off*).   My Prince !

Simple Simon (*teasingly, to* Red Riding Hood). He's *her* Prince now—not yours !

Red Riding Hood.   You silly boy !   He's *my* Prince.   The Good Fairy said so.   I believe in my Good Fairy !

(*Cue for a song.   Music strikes up.*)

Simple Simon.   If you're going to make a song and dance about it, I'm off !

(*He exits* r.)

(*Song by* Red Riding Hood.)

(*Enter* Mrs. Hubbard, *sobbing.   She is using a handkerchief with a very loud and gaudy pattern.*)

Red Riding Hood.   Why, Mother dear, whatever *is* the matter ?

Mrs. Hubbard (*trying to appear controlled*).   Oh nothing, my dear.   Just having a rinse down, that's all.   (*She squeezes out her handkerchief.*)

Red Riding Hood.   But you're crying !

Mrs. Hubbard.   Am I really ?   (*She gulps.*) Good gracious me, so I am !   (*She gulps.*)   I—I—I wondered what was the matter.

Red Riding Hood (*going to her*).   What ails you, Mother ?

Mrs. Hubbard.   It's not ale, my dear.   It's too salt for that.

(Mrs. Hubbard *holds up the handkerchief and surveys the pattern with amazement.*)

Has all that come out of my eyes ?

Red Riding Hood.   Don't worry, Mother.   That's only the pattern.   Mother, why are you crying ?   Is it something the Prince said ?

Mrs. Hubbard (*sobbing again*).   It's not what he *said*.   What he *said* was beautiful—beautiful.   It —it's what he didn't say that's—well—that's upset me.   Feel in my pocket, darling, and you'll find my smelling-salts.   I'm feeling a little faint.

(Red Riding Hood *finds a bottle in* Mrs. Hubbard's *pocket.*)

Red Riding Hood (*reading the label*).   Is *this* it ? It's marked " Brandy."

Mrs. Hubbard (*snatching the bottle*).   That's it ! There's no need to shout it out.   (*Embarrassed.*)   In any case, I—I only *smell* it.   I never drink the stuff.

(*She turns her back to the audience and has a drink. She faces front again, taking care to be wiping her nose and not her lips.*)

It's—it's *you*—not *me* !   To think that he wants to marry *you*—a mere babe in arms.   My dream is shattered.   I shall never be the same again.   (*She looks at the bottle.*) Yes—the same again ! (*She turns and has another drink.*)

(*Enter the* Footman, r.)

Footman. His Royal Highness wishes to see the young lady.

Mrs. Hubbard. Well—there are two of us !

Footman. The—er—*young* lady, madam.

Mrs. Hubbard (*indignant*). And how old d'you think *I* am ?

Footman (*cautiously*). I have really no idea, madam.

Mrs. Hubbard (*nudging him*). Go on ! Give a guess !

Footman. I should say—about forty-five, madam —since you press me !

Mrs. Hubbard. I'm sorry I pressed him ! Well, go along, my dear. You mustn't keep the Prince waiting. Let me take a look at you. (*She inspects her dress.*) Yes, you look very nice. I think you'll do me credit.

Red Riding Hood. I'm not going away for good, Mother. Who knows—I may come back shortly— crying, like you !

Mrs. Hubbard. If you do, you shan't have any of my smelling-salts. There won't be any left. (*She looks at the bottle.*) I've very nearly smelt it all away !

Red Riding Hood (*going off* r.). Good-bye, Mother !

Mrs. Hubbard. Good-bye, my darling—and— good health (*she corrects herself*)—I—I mean—good luck !

(*Exit* Red Riding Hood, r.)

Footman (*eyeing the bottle with disdain*). The bar is on your right, madam !

Mrs. Hubbard. Thank you. I'll have a smell of that presently.

(*Exit the* Footman, r. *Enter the* Baron, *back* o. *He has a paper in his hand and is very elated.*)

BARON. Mrs. Hubbard, I have something important to say to you!

MRS. HUBBARD. If you've come for the rent again, Baron, this is not the time—or the place!

BARON. I owe you an apology. Never again will I make such demands on you. See, here is a paper, signed by me, in which I waive all claim to arrears of rent. (*He waves the paper in front of her face.*)

MRS. HUBBARD. Why all this flag-wagging?

BARON. My lands are free from the menace of the wolves. King Wolf is dead. I walk on air!

MRS. HUBBARD. I wish you'd teach me how to do that. It would ease my corns a lot!

BARON. I am a new man!

(MRS. HUBBARD *takes out her lorgnettes.*)

MRS. HUBBARD. If you're a *new* man, I must take a good look. I certainly didn't like the old one. (*She gazes at him through the glasses.*) Yes, the new model is certainly an improvement.

(*The heads of* PUNCH *and* TRUNCH *are seen peering round the entrance back* C.)

PUNCH. There he is!

(PUNCH *and* TRUNCH *enter quickly and place themselves one on each side of the* BARON.)

We've got you, now!

MRS. HUBBARD. What is the matter, Officer?

PUNCH. He's under arrest for trying to steal your daughter.

MRS. HUBBARD. There must be some mistake. The man who's trying to do that is in there. (*She points* R.) His name is Prince Charming—and he has my full permission! (*Aside.*) I should say so!

PUNCH. Prince Charming?

TRUNCH. Blimey!

PUNCH. 'Struth!

BARON (*smiling confidently*).   Are you satisfied now, Sergeant ?

PUNCH.   I'm s-sorry you've been troubled.

(TRUNCH *reaches up and hits* PUNCH *on the head.*)

TRUNCH.   You're a *nice* policeman !

(TRUNCH *runs off back* C.   PUNCH *gives a howl of rage and pursues him.   They exit back* C.)

MRS. HUBBARD (*coyly*).   I wish some nice strong man would steal me !

BARON (*bowing*).   May I have that privilege, madam ?

MRS. HUBBARD.   Oh, Baron, this is so sudden.

(*She flings herself into his arms.   Enter* DANDY, R.)

DANDY.   I'm so sorry.   Perhaps I should have knocked before coming in, but there aren't any doors to knock on.

MRS. HUBBARD (*pretending to be unconcerned*).   Oh, it's quaite all raight !   We were only discussing one or two—er——

DANDY.   Affairs of state.   I know !

MRS. HUBBARD.   Er—yes.   The Baron and I have just entered into an alliance.

BARON.   A pact of non-aggression !

MRS. HUBBARD.   Oh—more than that !   We're going to get married !

BARON (*aghast at her precipitancy*).   *What !*

MRS. HUBBARD.   Baron—I trust I haven't taken the very words out of your mouth ?

BARON.   Not at all.   They hadn't even entered my head.

MRS. HUBBARD (*patting him playfully*).   Ah !   You old pretender !   You can't deceive me !   Let us go and celebrate.

(*She steers the* BARON *towards the buffet off* R.)

BARON.   You certainly don't let the grass grow under your feet.

Mrs. Hubbard. No, Baron. There's no grass about me. I'm not that sort of a widow.

(*Exit* Mrs. Hubbard *and* Baron.)

Dandy. That's an enterprising family. Mother and daughter both doing well. There's going to be a marriage boom, if I'm not much mistaken. Hubbards are getting on—and I must be getting off. But how ?

> Well, marriage-mongers all may scoff,
> But a song and dance will get *me* off !

(*Song and dance by* Dandy, *assisted by the* Chorus. *who remain on after the number.*)

(*The* Chorus *dress the stage* R. *and* L. *for the cabaret, This cabaret can be introduced as a means of bringing on any special turns that may be available. The* Chorus *should assist in the capacity of audience, applauding the various numbers. After the cabaret the* Prince *and* Red Riding Hood *appear at the archway, back* C. *The* Prince *leads* Red Riding Hood *down the steps.*
> *Fanfare and cheers.*)

Prince. If you don't know what has happened,
> you can guess.
I asked her if she would—and she said : " Yes."

(*More cheers from the* Chorus, *during which* Mrs. Hubbard *and the* Baron *push their way to* C.)

Mrs. Hubbard. There's something more to guess
> before you go.
I asked *him* if *he* would and he said——
Baron. *No !*
Mrs. Hubbard. But I just wouldn't take *no* for an answer, so we're going to be married too. Cheers, please.

(*The* Chorus *cheer.*)

I thank you. (*She looks triumphantly at the* Baron.)
Carried unanimously !

(RED RIDING HOOD *steps forward to speak the
Epilogue.*)

RED RIDING HOOD.   Dear audience, before you go
away
There's just one little thing I've got to say.
For many years it's always been the vogue
To end the panto with an epilogue.
But when I try to thank you all in verse,
I just can't do it.   I get worse and worse!
How can I use a couplet and a rhyme
To say, " I hope you've had a happy time " ?
MRS. HUBBARD. Well, you've said it and it
rhymes, that's very good.
But I think you've said enough, Red Riding Hood.
Now you make way, you saucy little rogue,
And let your betters speak the epilogue.
Oh, I say, now, that's another rhyme!
How funny it should happen every time!
PRINCE.   I think, my friends, in case we should
make *you sick,*
We'd better say this epilogue—with *Music.*

GRAND FINALE.

9 780573 064364